# Marjorie Daingerfield

is a professional sculptress and former instructor in Sculpture at: School of American Sculpture, New York; Grand Central School of Art, New York; Guild Hall School of Art, East Hampton; Rollins College, Winter Park, Florida; Norton Gallery, School of Art, Palm Beach.

THE FUN
AND
FUNDAMENTALS
OF
SCULPTURE

# The Fun
## and Fundamentals
# OF SCULPTURE

BY MARJORIE JAY DAINGERFIELD

*New York*

CHARLES SCRIBNER'S SONS

731
P 182
Sculpture - Tecnique

*Dedicated*
*to my beloved husband*
*J. Louis Lundean*

# CONTENTS

# Chapter 1

## MODELLING THE HEAD

For years friends have been looking at my sculpture and saying, "Couldn't you tell others how to do it?" So now, I shall attempt to write down in some logical sequence some of the hows and whys of sculpture, hoping to be helpful to the beginner and refreshing to the professional.

I always find my students want to start out with the head—short of a kindergarten group, no one is interested in rolling out a carrot or a banana. What people are always interested in is personality. You have always in a group a little narcissus—one who wants to do himself—"Here I was at this time and this is how I looked"—but usually there is someone beloved who must be given immortality—an earthly variety, but sculpture is the most permanent of the arts. This can be thrilling or distressing, as the case may be.

Let us then consider first the head—and here I must commit a heresy from the point of view of the present-day abstractionist or extreme modernist. I believe the human head is based on the human skull—not an old egg-beater, a sucked lollipop, or a doughnut—so if the student is willing to draw and draw and draw again the skull, from all views, there is the best basis for a head—knowledge of the underlying bone structure. After a while, because of its wonderful

SKULL
from the front

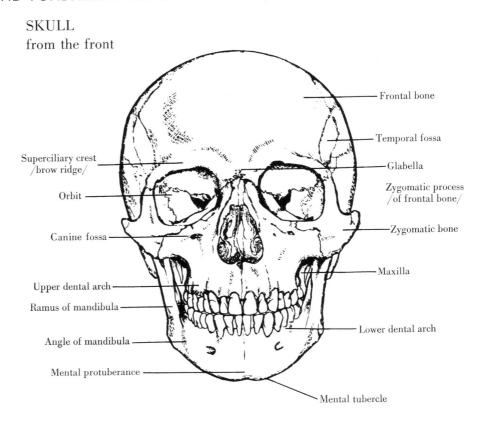

Frontal bone

Temporal fossa

Glabella

Zygomatic process
/of frontal bone/

Zygomatic bone

Maxilla

Lower dental arch

Mental tubercle

Superciliary crest
/brow ridge/

Orbit

Canine fossa

Upper dental arch

Ramus of mandibula

Angle of mandibula

Mental protuberance

perfection, the functional necessity of every bone, it becomes an object of beauty.

Having then acquired some knowledge of eye sockets—the angle of the cheekbone—the jawbone—the elevation of the brow above the eyes—you are ready to start your modelling, and you are starting something you will probably never give up, because sculpture takes you up—you don't take it up—and it's a joyous addiction. I have at times tried

from the left side

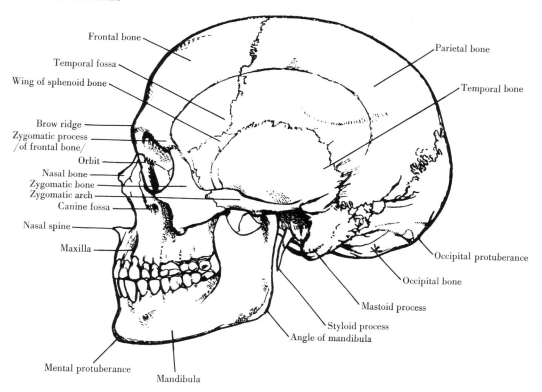

Frontal bone

Temporal fossa

Wing of sphenoid bone

Parietal bone

Temporal bone

Brow ridge
Zygomatic process
/of frontal bone/
Orbit
Nasal bone
Zygomatic bone
Zygomatic arch
Canine fossa
Nasal spine
Maxilla

Mental protuberance

Mandibula

Angle of mandibula

Styloid process

Mastoid process

Occipital bone

Occipital protuberance

to drop it, tossed my tools in the garbage, gone to Florida—
only to find myself sitting on somebody's beach piling up
wet sand.

To begin with, you need clay—or plasteline. Clay has
to be kept moist, but plastilina contains an oil which keeps
it always in a workable condition—about 50 lbs. for a head.
Then you need an armature (see p. 13). It resembles the
middle wicket of a croquet set.

MATERIALS

11

To make an armature, get a four-by-five plywood board about 12″ x 14″. Put flanges under this to facilitate picking it up—also, if you are using wet clay, it prevents your board from warping. Nail to this a square piece of wood about eight inches high—nail to center of board. Get about a yard of lead wire, which is strong but pliable. Bend as shown and nail to wood. If you use wet clay, it must be kept wrapped in moist rags, and cover these with a piece of thin plastic cloth fastened together with clothespins. This keeps the air out and the clay from cracking. Do not have your rags too wet— wring out so they are moist. Some sculptors make a light- weight box such as an apple crate lined with flannel, which they spray with a garden sprayer, and set this down over the head instead of wrapping it—this is a good way too. For using plastilina, no wetting is necessary, so it is easier, though it does not work up as rapidly.

I will never forget one time when I went to Richmond, Virginia, to give a talk on sculpture to the Women's Club and a demonstration of how to model a head. I had my armature in a little crate on the train with me. As I got off, I said to

*Opposite:* An armature

the porter, handing him the crate, "Handle this gently," and a lady standing by me said, "Oh, the dear little thing. I didn't hear a sound out of it all night!"

Tools for the beginner need not be too numerous. A few such as these will be sufficient, although there are tools for every imaginable use. The best tools are your fingers. It is very helpful, particularly to the student who hasn't an instinctive feeling for proportion, to have a pair of calipers.

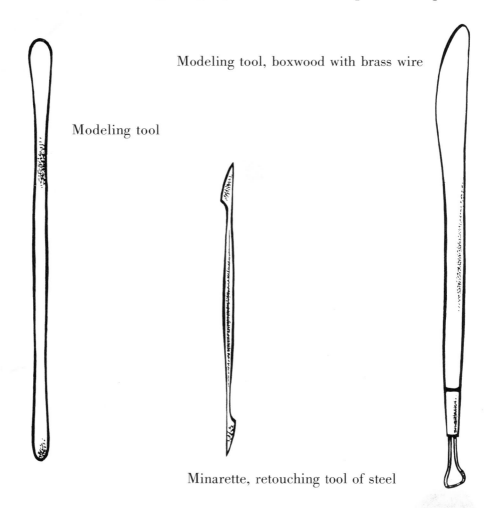

Modeling tool, boxwood with brass wire

Modeling tool

Minarette, retouching tool of steel

14

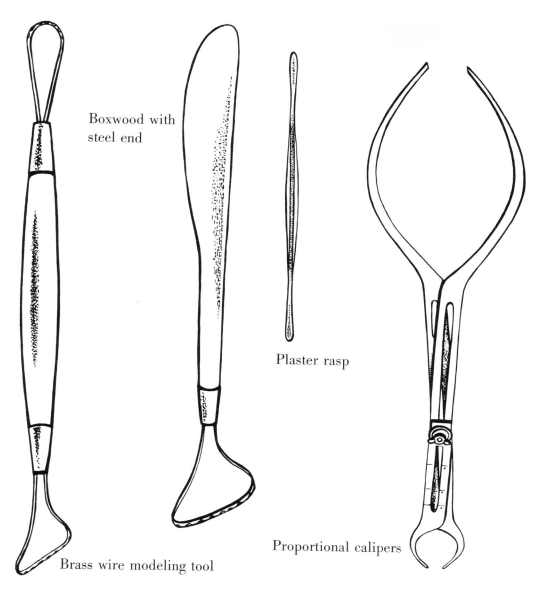

Boxwood with
steel end

Plaster rasp

Brass wire modeling tool

Proportional calipers

You will have to have a modelling stand which rotates, and your sitter should be placed on a model stand which rotates, at eye level. Your stand will raise up and down. Such stands may be purchased at an art supply store for about $25.00—or made of wood by a local carpenter for less.

15

STUDIO

The painter has the advantage over us. He has to cope with only one view and can depend on the same light and shade, while the sculptor has to get the likeness all around, from every view, and the light and shade will always be different. It has to be good from every side and in every light.

The ideal studio has plenty of room, a good steady north light, preferably an overhead light or skylight. Protect your floor with some kind of covering—sculpture is a messy job and will drip. Sculptors are not as dependent on a north light as painters. Because changing light is vital, you must turn your work often—not work in any one light—not in a strong light. Walk away—back from your work—so that the detail is lost in the big masses—the big directions—the large movement of planes. Distance thus lends enchantment or disenchantment—according to how accurate your observation of your work is. It is very valuable to have a large mirror on one wall so that you can see two sides or front and back of your sitter at once. You will have to learn to work anywhere—in somebody's parlor or—as I did—out on an Indian reservation outdoors. To have ideal conditions is not essential—but wonderful if you can achieve them.

THE HEAD

If you live in New York or other cities where you see great skyscrapers going up, you will note that the underlying first steel structure gives you the big outlines of the ultimate building. No decoration or elaboration alters the big general planes of the building—only conforms to it. So in starting

16

your head, overlook detail. Start with the big masses, the big movements of form, the simple planes. A plane is a flat surface, like the side of a cube.

Every individual has a typical way of holding his head—some forward, some very erect, some to one side. The

17

characteristic poise of the head on the neck is essential to the final likeness, so before you begin to pile on clay, study this carriage of the head carefully and bend your armature accordingly. Most students make the back of the head and the neck on a straight line. This never happens. If you have studied your skull, you know it sets forward at quite an angle from the seventh cervical vertebra. (See p. 20.)

Having gotten the big lines of direction—the pose of the head—start from a side view and build up a thin layer of clay to give you an outline of the skull. Turn it front view and fill out the width. Put in the big frontal plane of the brow, the cheeks, and the planes running back to the ears. Fill in the back of the skull, remembering that there is as much behind the ears as in front!—just as important.

Now everyone has eyes, ears, a mouth and nose. It is how these features are placed in relation to each other and to the *whole mass of the skull* that makes the difference between people.

The features, then, can be called elaboration or detail. They do not destroy or interrupt the basic structure of the head—they conform to it—and if the skull is correct in its proportion, they will fall into place like the last pieces in a jigsaw puzzle—and they *have* to be right. Right down to the bone, back of any features exists a plane which I call the facial angle. Here there are only three possibilities—it is a perpendicular plane (the classic), or a concavity (Bob Hope,

Mussolini), or a convexity (with a retreating chin). Look around you and see how everyone falls into one of the three broad categories. Make up your mind which your sitter belongs in. Get that.

Now you are ready to put in the eye sockets. Do you remember their shape from your drawings? Now put on a mass, a plane roughly to indicate the shape your nose will ultimately take. Sculpture builds outward; it grows like a flower—don't try to get any one feature right and leave it— it is only right insofar as it is in relation to all the forms and from every view. Keep turning your work, turning your model. Everything is in a state of flux, of growing, of change —it must develop all over equally. Do not finish one part too far. The sooner you are able to see all over the head at once, the faster you will learn to model one. The nose is right only as it is placed in relation to the ear, to the eyes, to the mouth, chin, etc. See it all as a unity—do not think of one section at a time.

I will take the various features up separately now to try to tell you how to go about modelling them because I am limited to words. But if I were there with you, I would show you how necessary it is to work at one feature while you are observing its relation to another. To balance one side with another, draw a line actually with a tool down the center of the head and keep balancing across—one feature with another. You may also find it helpful to take a few simple

19

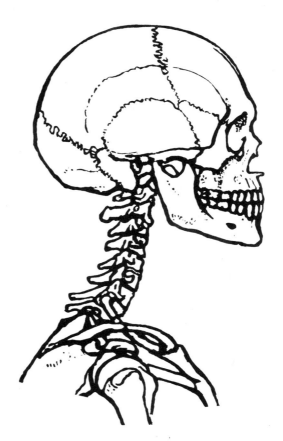

measurements with your calipers—from the top of the skull to the chin—from ear to ear—and through the width from back to front. You can make these measurements visible from all sides by sticking in matchsticks which project and can be kept in place.

THE EYES     To start modelling the eyes, dig in your eye sockets. The eye is a round ball which sets down in the socket, being protected from harm by a ridge of bone all around—the frontal bone always projects far beyond the eyeball. Now lay on the lids, which conform to the round contour of the eyeball

—the outer corner is always higher than the inner corner. The expression of the eye is attained by studying the forms around it—not in the eyeball itself. There are many ways of suggesting the iris. Houdon, the great French sculptor, makes a spiral form. The Greeks, of course, left the form of the eyeball round—simple—with no indication of undercuts for the iris or pupil. Often this blank look has given people the feeling that eyes in sculpture are expressionless. This is not true. Even the color of the eye can be indicated—the depth of shadow caused by cutting in deeply gives the illusion of a dark eye, while less deep undercuts which do not throw shadows will give an impression of light eyes. Leave a little wedge-shaped high spot on your eye to catch the light and serve as a highlight, giving luminosity to the eye.

There is a cast of an eye modelled by Michelangelo, which can be bought at any art supply store, that is valuable to copy. Hang it up so it is perpendicular—do not lay it flat to copy it, or it will confuse you as to relative depths of the corners of the eye. The most important things you will learn, you will find out for yourself—I am only hoping to make the road easier by pointing out the simple ways of getting results and how to avoid pitfalls.

THE MOUTH

In many years of teaching, I have found certain universal mistakes which almost all beginners make and when we come to modelling the mouth, let me warn you it is *never flat*. Most students draw on the mouth and make it flat. The

21

First sitting

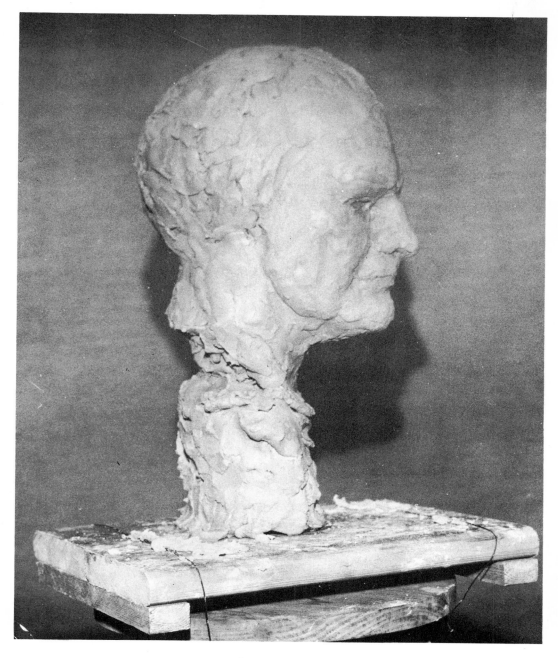

Second sitting

Nearing completion. Portrait of Mr. George M. Ivey by the author.

lips conform to the underlying shape of the teeth—which is round. When you bite into a sandwich, you bite a curve—the corners of the mouth are deeper in than the center. Now the mouth divides into five forms—the upper lip two ovals on the sides, one round form in the center, the lower lip into two long ovals. Do not be afraid to go in deeply for the corners. Study them carefully, as here exists one of the salient points for likeness. Often a tiny ridge is left, indicating a change of plane for the lips and by casting a tiny shadow—a change of color. The mouth has so much mobility, usually too much, as your sitter will talk to you, so that it is a matter of selecting what mood the mouth shall express. The line between the lips is more uniform in depth—not a cold, hard line—but one of varying depths and moving play of light and shade. Sometimes, particularly with children, a breathing look can be captured by leaving the lips slightly parted.

THE NOSE

The most immobile and yet the most characterful feature of the face is the nose. Here is seen ancestry, nationality, and individuality. It is divided into three distinct planes —one in the center, one down each side. The shape of the nostrils, how they flare, is important to observe, and the ridge between the nostrils—whether it is thin or wide—defines the shape of the nostrils. Watch this form carefully from below—do not dig in the nostril too deep. An unnecessarily dark shadow in the nostrils detracts from a concentration of

25

interest in the eyes. The upper lip usually attaches mid-way of the width of the nose—most pupils attach the upper lip too far back. The outline of the nose in profile never meets the upper lip at a sharp angle. There is a small plane dividing the two, and this gives a quality of life to the silhouette.

THE EAR    The ear is the most difficult feature to model. Where it is placed in the head is most important. It is the point from which you measure the distance to the nose, mouth, fore-head, and chin. The cheekbone runs into the eardrum. The axis of the ear is usually parallel to the angle of the nose. Usually the top of the ear is on a line with the eyebrows and the lobe on a line drawn from the nostrils. The distance that the ear stands out from the head is important too. There is a tendency to make the ear too flat. The back view has to be modelled.

At Rollins, I had a student who had *demountable* ears on his first head. He would model the ear in his hand, and on both sides, then stick it on the head, first on one side and then the other, to see which way it looked best. It looked terrible both ways. The ear has to seem to grow out of the head, and cannot be modelled separately and stuck on. The convolutions of the ear are interesting to study, as they differ in every individual. It is the variant from the norm that gives character, and capturing it makes sculpture exciting.

THE HAIR    For modelling the hair you must use imagination.
26    Taste, design, rhythm play a part in how you decide to treat

hair, but you will observe the hair does grow in a pattern, layer upon layer. At the crown of the head is a swirl or a spiral that lends interest to the top and back of the head. Where the hair grows from the brow, the undercuts should be very soft—let them merge gently into the face. A sharp hard line gives the effect of a wig. Where there is a high-light on the hair, leave it smooth to catch the light. Scratches on the surface do not make hair that is convincing. Study the way it grows, the rhythm of a wave, the soft shadow occa-sioned by a curl—make the levels distinct and you will find there is an underlying pattern. Hair can be done with imagi-nation. You can make an unseen wind blow it. Above all, do not make the part so deep that it goes below the level of the contour of the skull—part the hair with a comb and not with a meat axe.

THE CUT-OFF

Where you terminate your head is a matter of taste also. You can go on and do full shoulders or cut it off mid-way of the shoulder or at the base of the neck—wherever the line seems to add to the rhythm of the composition as a whole. There is no arbitrary rule as to where to stop. You can keep on as long as your energy and clay hold out but when you do decide, "This is as far as I will go," take a wire or sharp tool and cut it off there—make it definite. Don't just let your clay dribble off in an indefinite manner into nothingness. The final designing of the cut-off can enhance a head greatly or detract from it.

27

# Chapter 2

## SCULPTURE IN RELIEF

There are two types of relief—one low or "bas relief," the other "haut" or high relief. Bas relief is satisfying in the way the science of mathematics is. It is absolutely logical and the result is entirely accurate or it is entirely wrong. There are no half measures. Bas relief, like drawing, requires a knowledge of foreshortening and equally the effect of light and shade is important. Primitive peoples who also had in common with us "the Kilroy complex"—"Here I was at this time and this is what I saw"—made a record by scratching on the walls of caves with sharp stones what was really a bas relief. The majestic reliefs of the Egyptian who had no knowledge of fore-shortening were so suited to the perpendicular lines of the terrain of Egypt that they conform to their environment. In their use of a pattern of light and shade and in their depiction of life itself they have not been surpassed.

Today, however, we are supposed to know the principles of fore-shortening and to be able to draw. Bas relief is a drawing in clay. A bas relief is a gradual retrogression—a telescoping of planes.

I think a good way to describe the retreating of planes in a relief is to think of an open fan—let each section of the fan represent a plane. As you slowly close the fan the distances between the spokes lessen but the first one is still the highest. The next one is the next highest and so on. Their relation to each other remains the same—so with a bas relief.

To start a relief, have a good strong board, square or rectangular. Surround this with an edge of wood or framework which will be higher than the highest point of your relief. Make a smooth background of clay. To make it smooth quickly, I draw a ruler across it which cuts off any projections and makes any pits or holes obvious. Now, on this smooth surface make an outline drawing of your subject, say a head in profile and shoulders. The shoulder will be the thickest plane because it is nearer to you, then the ear. The other planes, like the folding fan, will retreat relatively into the background. Never allow any point, even the inner corner of the eye, which is on the lowest level, ever to go back below the level of the background. Cut away your background. You now see that you have the start of a relief. A relief is fascinating to work on; the play of light and shade changes it from one time to another. The center of the head is fuller than the sides which, on a curving plane, move into the background. The outline on a good relief is never of one continuous depth. It varies in depth with the form. It varies in direction and

29

North walls of the great Hypostyle Hall at Karnak. An Egyptian relief showing
incised outlines rather than raised relief.

Donatello's *David*

depth, losing itself behind or coming in front of another part. As some muscles move toward the back the outline goes deeper with it. As other muscles come to the front the outline fills and comes forward with it. The outline should never be one consistent elevation from the background but merge gently into the background at some points and be emphasized at others.

A relief is primarily a design against a background offering scope for the imagination and sense of pattern. An overelaboration of detail and cramming of forms into a relief is a fault. Do not crowd your work. The tendency among students in bas-relief modelling is to cut the hollows in too deeply and to raise the projections too high.

I usually have my board clamped tightly on an easel with a strong screw clamp so that I can stand or sit before it as you would in painting a canvas. It has happened that the clamp slipped and the board fell face-down on the floor. Instead of being a tragedy this is often a blessing. Any projections that have been modelled up on too high a level are flattened down by striking the floor and the planes are mashed back into their correct relationship.

Mr. Julio Kilenyi, who had a studio on the floor with mine in the "Hotel des Artistes," was a master at bas relief. A famous medallist, he had done reliefs so long that it seemed effortless. I would watch him, fascinated, as little worms of clay would roll off his fingers and become beautiful letters,

Paul Manship's
*Centaur and Dryad*

each on its perfect axis with the center of his medal. Lettering is a study in itself and requires time and effort. Mr. Kilenyi made his circular bas reliefs in a pie pan! It gave him the depth of clay he needed and maintained a perfect circle for him at all times. It is a great help to study photographs of the works of the masters of bas relief—Saint Gaudens, Paul Manship (what delicacy and mastery of technique and design!), Donald De Lue, to mention a few of our contemporaries.

From the practical angle it is good to be able to capture a likeness in relief as the cost is less. They hang on the wall and require less space than a head in the round, and there seems always to be a demand for them.

33

Lucy Gins. Portrait by the author. This marble head is modelled as though it were a bas relief, but it has two sides and the front view is only one-half inch in thickness. It gives the illusion of a head in the round.

Anne
Cannon
Reynolds,
by the author

A portrait is an interpretation. It is the artist—what he sees and feels—plus the sitter. The intangible quality of the spirit must be found and captured. An external observation alone has no life. It is the inner spirit looking out of the face that gives it life and lifts a portrait head into the realm of art.

In a book for students it is not necessary to go into the field of architectural relief although among you may lurk a great architectural sculptor. As you move about from one city to another, keep observing buildings which have sculptural ornamentation. It has, up to now, been felt that sculpture on a building should conform to the architectural lines of the building, but today in many modern buildings you will find very high reliefs which look as though they had been tossed from a distance and just stuck, through some miraculous form of adhesion, to the smooth surface of the building. These manifestations are supposed to take away from the stark simplicity of a blank wall and to be ornamentations. I often wonder if they are.

Delicacy of detail may be achieved by working with a sharp steel instrument in reverse, in the plaster mold. In a mold the high points are the low ones when cast and the low ones are the high points, like the light and shade in a negative. It is easier to do lettering, for instance, by digging into the mold than by adding on clay and raising them up. Many more details or inequalities are brought out by studying the mold than can be observed in the cast.

The technique of modelling in relief comes to you gradually. Keep trying and eventually, like learning to ride a bicycle, you'll be able to get both feet off the ground and roll! Don't let a few failures discourage you. In fact, when it comes to sculpture, so many unforeseen things can arise that you have to learn to eliminate the word *discouragement* from your mind.

The greatest lesson I ever had in overcoming discouragement happened in San Juan, Puerto Rico. I had gone there to model the head of Dr. Bailey K. Ashford. He was a very great and wonderful man and had cured so many thousands of cases of Sprue and hookworm and other tropical diseases that he was the idol of the island. He was a great scientist as well as an inspired and dedicated doctor, but he was very near the end himself and, of course, knew it. He was a Colonel in the U.S. Army and wore the uniform when he sat for me, which he did with the fortitude of an officer and a gentleman though in great pain and having to take morphine to be able to pose.

After several weeks of work, I had the head completed but still in the wet clay, when I received a letter from the Governor. He wrote that he had heard that the bust of the great Dr. Ashford had been done and he would like to be invited to see it—to bring the Press and the photographers and give it some publicity. This was a Royal Command!

I appointed eleven o'clock on a never-to-be-forgotten Thursday morning for the Governor to come to see the head, this being the coolest time of the day. That Thursday morning I was awakened by hearing a terrific crash that shook the house. Emerging from my mosquito-net-draped bed, I tottered downstairs and found that the native servant, in slicking up

37

for the Governor, had run his vacuum cleaner into the stand and there was my head, buttered over the floor. All that was left of my beautiful head was a forlorn, bent wire! I am told that I said, "I want my mama." At any rate, I fell on the sofa in a flood of tears. Finally I got up the courage to phone Dr. Ashford and tell him something dreadful had happened. He came right over and I can see him now, as he stood in the doorway, so tall, so handsome, surveying the scene. Then he walked over to me, as I lay sobbing on the sofa, his blue eyes blazing, and he said, "Virginia aristocracy doesn't mean anything, does it? You want everybody on this island to think you're a hit-and-miss sculptor? You could do this thing once, but you can't do it again? Now you scrape that stuff off the floor, begin again, do it better this time. I'm sitting for you right now!" I had never been talked to in that way before but was so ashamed to think that Dr. Ashford, old and dying, had more courage than I did. I knew, too, that there is no formula in art, two and two don't always make four. I didn't know if I could do it again or not, but I got down on my knees and started scraping up the clay off the floor.

In the meantime Dr. Ashford's charming British son-in-law, Maurice Guimess, had come in and knew the sad state of affairs, so when the whine of motorcycle out-riders and the fanfare that accompanies the arrival of the Governor was heard, Maurice was at the door to greet him with the

Dr. Bailey K. Ashford, by the author

inimitable diplomacy which the English always seem able to come up with in times of crisis. This is the conversation I heard through the open French doors: "Good morning, Governor, lovely day, what? But women, Governor, always a problem, aren't they, and a woman who is an artist doubly a problem. Today, Governor, Miss Daingerfield is in one of those moods they get in. Seems there's a little something more she wants to do to the head before you see it! Do you mind awfully? Will call you one day next week."

I, of course, listened to him in complete horror. A little something more I wanted to do to it!

I started in to work. This time, miraculously, effortlessly, the head seemed to build itself up. In six days I had it finished and now I had the soldier! I had seen the unconquerable spirit rising superior over any weakness of the flesh. The second head *was* better than the first. When the news broke about the first head being destroyed, there were such headlines in the paper! They almost had civil war as to who would present the bust. The Medical Association wanted to give it. The Ashford family wanted to give it. Finally, they passed an act of legislature and the Government bought it. Now the bronze stands in the hall of the School of Tropical Medicine, San Juan, where fresh flowers are kept in front of it in memory of a very great man. There is also a replica of it in Georgetown University, Washington, D.C., where a room is dedicated in Dr. Ashford's memory, and another bronze was unveiled in 1961 in a great public school in Brooklyn, New York, named in his honor.

So do not be discouraged. What, at the moment, may seem a tragedy can, in reality, be a valuable lesson and a blessing.

# Chapter 3

## MODELLING THE FIGURE

THE POSE
AND THE
ARMATURE

To model the human figure convincingly, it is important to have a knowledge of underlying bone structure and anatomy. *Gray's Anatomy* is one of the best books on the subject. Then, when you have the opportunity to work in a life class, you will know what you are looking at. An external observation of a model is not enough for the sculptor. He must know what causes what he sees. Certain bones always emerge to the surface and can be called points of attachment for here muscles attach and varying planes of motion start. The collar bones, the sternum, the elbows, the knees, the spine, the crest of the pelvic bone, the ankles, these are bones you can readily see regardless of the weight of your model or how little you know of anatomy. These you can recognize and they will be anchors in whatever sea of uncertainty.

As with the head, so with the figure. You must begin with a good substantial armature; if you don't, you'll come in some morning to find your gay, uplifted dancing figure has become one of grief with the head bowed to the knees!

You can make your armature any size. Start with a square board a couple of inches thick (this can be made of plywood if necessary). At one side of it screw in a circular flange. In it put an iron pipe (small diameter) which will rise to the height of what you intend to be the small of the back. Then an "elbow" and another shorter pipe ending in a hollow "T." In this make a skeleton of lead wire. (See p. 44.) Do not have the legs meet the board as you will probably be shifting the weight and position. Many sculptors hang tiny little butterflies from the torso and the pelvic bone. However, I never felt these necessary; they get in my way and give me butterflies in the stomach. A butterfly is made of two crossed pieces of wood wired together and is intended to keep clay from slipping.

The first time I ever went to Art School I was in a life class of Mr. Solon Borglum. There was no instructor there, but a beautiful nude model in a graceful pose stood on the stand. I was told by the students to build an armature. Of course I had never heard of one and knew nothing about it, but with the help of some sympathetic pupils I built one and started in to work with wild enthusiasm. Two weeks passed. I had worked hard. My statue was to me a dream of beauty. Finally the great day came when Mr. Borglum came in to criticize his class. My heart was beating fast when he finally came to me. He looked at my work and said, "Miss Daingerfield, you think that's pretty good, don't you?" "Well," I said, "I don't think it's too bad." "Do you know what I think of

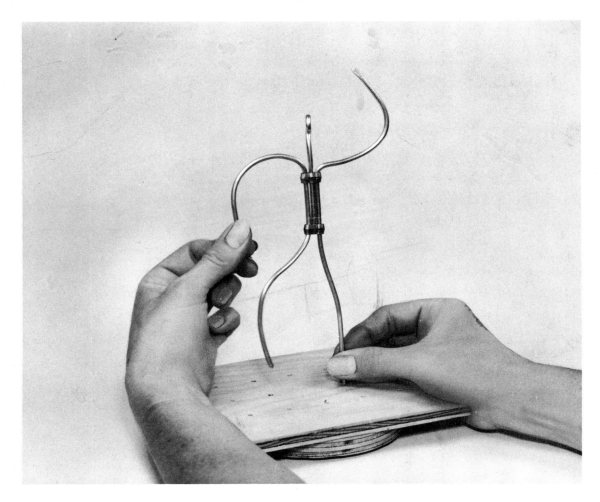

Figure armature

it?" *Pow,* and with two great fists he mashed it flat. That was the way he weeded out his class—if you burst into tears, you'd never be a sculptor, but if you got mad and started in to work then he was behind you, guiding and helping to the end. A wonderful teacher and in after years, realizing the many struggles, disillusionments, accidents that occur on the road to sculpture, I have been so grateful for that lesson in courage. Casts that lose detail, bubbles that form in a kiln, breakage in shipping, commissions that die a-borning—these are among the hazards to expect and surmount—and greatest of all the fact that your own work, completed to the limit of your capability, never equals the vision in your mind when you start.

After you have selected the pose which you wish your model to take, make chalk marks around her feet on the stand so that she can always return to the same position. Study the pose from every angle so that you can close your eyes and have a clear mental picture of the pose. Then start to pile your clay (or plasteline) on firmly so that it will not slip up and down. Most students have a mental impression of the spine as a perfectly straight bone. The spine is a series of curves. (See p. 46.) The action of the spine determines that of the whole figure, the front following the direction of the back. The undulating line of the spine can best be studied from a side view. The height of the adult figure is about 7½ to 8

45

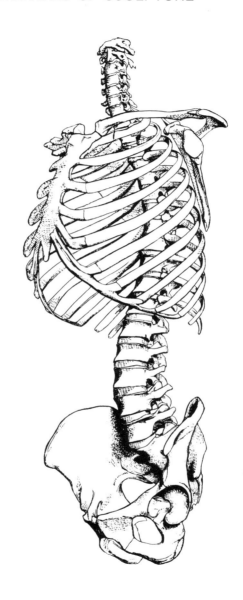

"The spine is a series of curves."

heads; of course with a child the head is larger in proportion to the body.

Be sure that your figure looks as though it were standing, maintaining its own weight on one or both legs. The pelvic bone will tip according to which leg sustains the most weight, that side being higher. The pelvic bone, when one is walking, rotates with very much the motion of a boat rocking on the water. First one side is high, then the other. If you drop a plumb line down from the pit of the throat it will fall directly on the inside ankle bone of the leg that supports the weight. Check your statue with the plumb line, be sure the balance of weight is maintained. As you work, you will suddenly become aware of a wonderful rhythm that plays through the whole figure. The planes move in a rhythmical direction. (See p. 48.) Study your figure all around, turning it constantly. Never become fascinated with modelling one section, as it is only right in its relation to the whole. Walk away from your work, get a perspective on it. Do not work standing too close to your work. The distant view gives you your work in its entirety, not one section at a time. The body is divided into two halves. As you work on one side see what happens on the corresponding side; as you work on the front be sure of what is happening on the back.

In classic sculpture the lower legs are made equal to the length of the upper leg. This proportion gives elegance to the figure. It is not often found today in the average model

BALANCE
OF
WEIGHT

PROPORTION

47

Note the rhythmical flow of line in the Cyrene Venus

but when found adds grace to the figure. Doubtless women are aware of this fact; hence the high heels which give a look of length to the lower leg and distinction to the figure as a whole.

There is probably no joy equal to the joy of creation. Painting is representation, music is often just interpretation, but sculpture is creation. To take a meaningless lump of clay, to see it begin to assume shape, the feel of it in your hands as you put it on in the direction which the planes you are observing take, to begin to see rhythm, motion, life evolve—here is a thrill those who never try it never know. Here you have a chance to express what you think or feel. The model vanishes, the idea is born! Suddenly you want your little figure to express something, to mean something, to say something that eludes the power of words.

How many sorrows are buried in clay, how many anxieties, how many problems? Here your mind is so concentrated, the awesome beauty of nature, so elusive to capture, so ever hauntingly present, reveals itself to you gradually, and the world with its disillusionments, its injustices, its wars and rumors of wars, fades into the background and your heart is filled with what can only be called the peace of God, since with His help—if you can add just a little to the beauty and the wonder of the world—you have fulfilled the mission given the artist. You have at least the illusion of significance.

49

Even a quietly standing figure must have the look of life, of latent motion. To learn to do a figure in action it is very helpful to have the model change position every twenty minutes and make quick action sketches—draw them if you can—or make quick clay studies. These little sketches will train your powers of observation and teach you the action of muscles in motion. Simply to make small wire armatures and bend them into positions of violent action is helpful since the underlying motion is expressed by the skeleton itself. The detail, the ultimate modelling of the figure, should not change or interrupt the action explicit in the position of the skeleton. It is very helpful to make collections of photographs which appeal to you. Magazines and newspapers, with the fast-lens camera of today, furnish infinite studies of the human body in action and of animals, capturing positions that actually elude the human eye. Skiing, diving, running, dancing—there are limitless opportunities to study the figure in motion. Also, in the field of sports, I think there is a great opportunity for the sculptor to design trophies. Some of the golf trophies and swimming trophies I have seen add horror to victory. Can there be anything uglier than an Oscar? In the field of achievement in the theater and motion pictures, a small statuette of the winner in his winning role would be so much more valued, so much more individual, and would give scope for the imagination and be such fun to do. I never enjoyed doing anything more than the statuette I did of Dorothy

Stickney as Vinnie in *Life with Father;* also one I did of Judith Evelyn as Mrs. Manningham in *Angel Street.*

In a free-standing single figure, remember that the silhouette is important. It will be viewed from all sides, it must carry at a distance. There must be a symmetry and a rhythm of line from every view. As you work be sure to walk well back often so that you can study the silhouette from a distance and from all sides. Also remember to change the light frequently; let it come first from one direction, then another. You will find your work looks best from an eye-level angle with an overhead light which casts shadows and brings out the modelling—but if it is your happy destiny to sell your sculpture, the purchaser will not know this and you will find your statue standing on a coffee table or on the TV set.

THE
SILHOUETTE

It is not my intention in this little book to teach anatomy; however, I do not want to fail to emphasize that for the serious student a background of knowledge of anatomy is essential. There are many wonderful books on the subject, any one of which would be helpful—Mr. George Bridgman's *Constructive Anatomy,* Sir Arthur Thompson's *Handbook of Anatomy for Art Students,* Gray's *Anatomy* among them.

Sculpture has always permeated my thinking to such an extent that even at the seashore I have thought of the sea as the drapery for the earth. Sometimes it casts a gossamer, lacy shawl over the shoulders of the earth and waves rolling in are great folds. As you practice modelling drapery you

DRAPERY

51

*Above:* Nike fragment, Palace of Athene

*Opposite:* Egyptian limestone, Yúny offering to Osiris

will feel the rhythm of the ocean, folds rolling in one direction, back in another, each following laws that are mystical or mathematical according to the way you feel about it. Truth is not altered by individual interpretations of it.

Drapery forms a vital part in sculpture. It gives solidity to the figure, it gives rhythm to the design, it gives motion. The varying ways in which drapery is designed and used and has been through the ages is a fascinating study. A repetition of line and majestic simplicity was achieved by the Egyptians in their handling of drapery. The Greeks gave rhythm and motion to the human figure. In the "Victory of Samothrace" an unseen wind forever blows, giving a forward, triumphant movement to the figure. In the "Three Graces" from the Parthenon, unity, rhythm, and beauty are achieved by the use of drapery. Here the figures are at once concealed and revealed. Drapery can do so much, can mean so much. In the great "Adams Memorial" by St. Gaudens in Washington, D.C., the dignity, the majesty, the mystery of the great brooding figure is achieved by the magnificent modelling of drapery.

To leave out the nonessential, to simplify to the greatest possible extent is a modern trend. A oneness is accomplished between the figure and the drapery by leaving out detail, by getting away from literal representation, by selecting and using only what is essential. Somewhat archaic in the derivation of this modern stylized method of modelling drapery,

The Adams Memorial by St. Gaudens. Massive folds of drapery give the figure dignity and meaning.

it is nonetheless effective, and far from easy. I would not suggest that the beginner try it. You have to have a knowledge of drapery and the forms it takes before you can eliminate the nonessential. The basic form remains. Then take away what is unimportant to the composition. You can't eliminate something that isn't there. You have to be like the little princess in the fairy story "who had read all the newspapers in the world, and forgotten them—so wise was she!"

To start studying how to model drapery, pin a sheet or any other piece of material up on something that allows you to see its full length, where the folds start and terminate.

Then, on a board, with your plasteline or clay start to copy it. You will find that different materials make very different folds. Folds of silk come to sharp points, folds of wool or velvet or a heavy material fall in rounded forms. It is fun to take a piece of damp cheesecloth, cover it with a layer of clay, and then lift it up and watch it fall into folds. You can experiment with draping a figure by placing such a clay-covered piece of material at various points to see where it looks best, where it adds to the composition. In modelling drapery on a figure do not cut so deeply that you cut into the figure. Remember, drapery is superimposed on the figure.

Observe that folds break around a central nucleus radiating in different directions from an obvious center. This somewhat spiral central point can be seen in any material and adds strength and authenticity to your modelling. The more you work at drapery, the more you will learn to leave out finicky little creases that do exist but do not add to the main big lines of the folds which must be part of your composition.

To differentiate between flesh and drapery, it is sometimes interesting to use a different finishing technique—to let tool marks remain on drapery gives a little roughness to the surface which can make a slight contrast with the smoothness of the handling of the flesh.

# Chapter 4

## ANATOMY

The principle which underlies the muscular structure in human anatomy, I think, can be best described to you by comparing it with Gothic architecture. If you look at a Gothic cathedral, or a picture of one, you will see that the great weight of the roof, pressing downward, would tend to cause the walls to collapse outward. This does not happen because of the flying buttresses which press inward from the outside, pushing the walls inward, thus counteracting the possibility of their falling outward. This, simply, is the principle known as counterthrust. Now this same principle works with the muscular structure. You will notice in a little baby the weight of the skull has a tendency to make the head fall forward. Its little back bends under the weight. The muscles are not developed enough to hold the back and head erect to exert a counteraction to the falling forward of the head. The same may be seen in a very old person where the erector muscles of the back have weakened. The back bends forward. The head leans forward because the muscles have lost the strength to hold the body erect.

Flying buttresses of Salisbury Cathedral

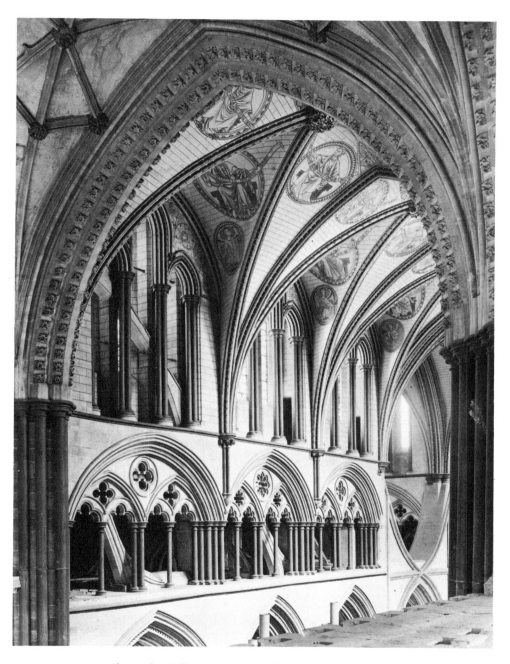

A vaulted Gothic arch in Salisbury Cathedral

Michelangelo exaggerated
muscle forms to emphasize
meaning.

I am not going into great detail on anatomy for you, just a broad outline of what I hope will be helpful. You could be the greatest anatomist in the world without being in any degree an artist. On the other hand you can not be an artist without some knowledge of anatomy, but remember anatomical details must be used to express the idea. Sculpture makes the idea visible. The actual perfection of knowledge of anatomy will not make a work of art. Michelangelo emphasized, exaggerated certain muscles to underscore the idea, to balance the composition, to make the design appear as he wished it to from the angle from which it was observed. Look at the attenuation of the Gothic sculpture made to conform to the soaring lines of the building on which it was placed. Use anatomy as a tool. Bend it to your will but never think that a mistake can be convincing. When you alter nature, do it deliberately.

Let us first consider the torso, the main and important muscles, and the spine, which influences from every angle the shape of the torso.

The rib cage is in the general shape of a barrel, the ribs being a protective shell for the vital organs. Study the general direction of the ribs. They slope downward in front, upward in the back. For the sculptor the bones that are visible, such as the sternum, the points of the scapula (or shoulder blade), the clavicle (or collarbone), make what I call points of attachment, which are always recognizable and visible from the surface. (See p. 64.)

The pelvic bone is roughly a basket. Remember what I told you in Chapter 2—the pelvic bone rotates like a boat on the water. As a person walks, his weight shifts from one leg to the other. The leg which maintains the weight is the higher. The ridge of the pelvic bone is a point of attachment. Where the leg bone, or femur, goes into the pelvis makes an indentation always visible and a point of attachment.

The scope of this little book does not include detailed anatomical plates but there are many, many books on anatomy which the student may study. For the beginner, I think, to have to learn long Latin names is slightly discouraging and boring. If you can learn the big movement and direction of muscles, I think this is sufficient because the more you learn the more you want to know. But to go into a detailed study of anatomy as a beginner might by its very minutae of detail detract from an instinctive sense of form and proportion and even impede an imaginative creative ability.

Since students always want to do heads it is very valuable and important to know something of the muscles of the neck. Remember the head always sets forward—never on a perfectly erect line—because the spine itself tips forward from the seventh cervical vertebra, which you can always see.

The most important and visible muscles which turn the head are the sterno cleido mastoid muscles which attach back of the ear and come forward and attach on the collarbones, thus forming a hollow called, usually, the pit of the throat. The carriage of the head on the shoulders is, remember, a

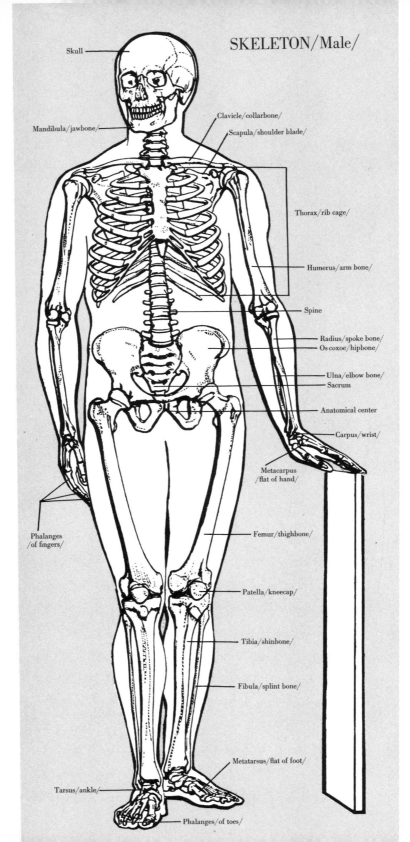

SKELETON/Male/

Skull

Mandibula/jawbone/

Clavicle/collarbone/

Scapula/shoulder blade/

Thorax/rib cage/

Humerus/arm bone/

Spine

Radius/spoke bone/
Os coxoe/hipbone/

Ulna/elbow bone/
Sacrum

Anatomical center

Carpus/wrist/

Metacarpus
/flat of hand/

Phalanges
/of fingers/

Femur/thighbone/

Patella/kneecap/

Tibia/shinbone/

Fibula/splint bone/

Metatarsus/flat of foot/

Tarsus/ankle/

Phalanges/of toes/

64

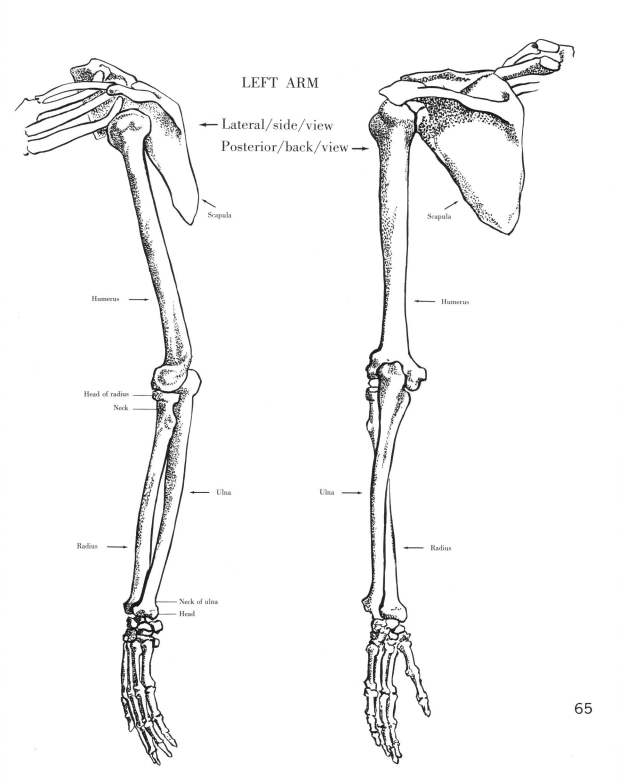

LEFT ARM

← Lateral/side/view

Posterior/back/view →

Scapula

Scapula

Humerus

Humerus

Head of radius

Neck

Ulna

Ulna

Radius

Radius

Neck of ulna

Head

65

most vital feature in getting a likeness. Everyone has a characteristic gesture of the head on the neck.

The arm has three bones—the humerus, the radius, the ulna. The radius rotates over the ulna. The two bones of the forearm are crossed when hanging down. The radius starting from the outer elbow bone passes along the ulna to the thumb side of the wrist. When we throw the arm outward, the palm of the hand up, the bones are parallel. (See p. 65.)

The hand has five metacarpal bones. It arches upward in the center. The great flexibility of the hand, its marvelous agility and infinity of uses, differentiates man from the animals who have no such tool, with the exception of the monkey,

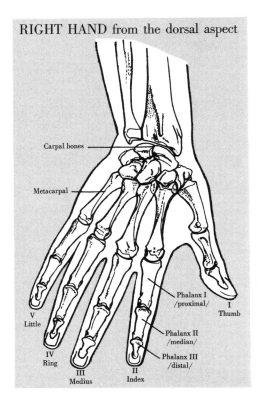

RIGHT HAND from the dorsal aspect

Carpal bones

Metacarpal

Phalanx I
/proximal/

I
Thumb

V
Little

Phalanx II
/median/

IV
Ring

Phalanx III
/distal/

III
Medius

II
Index

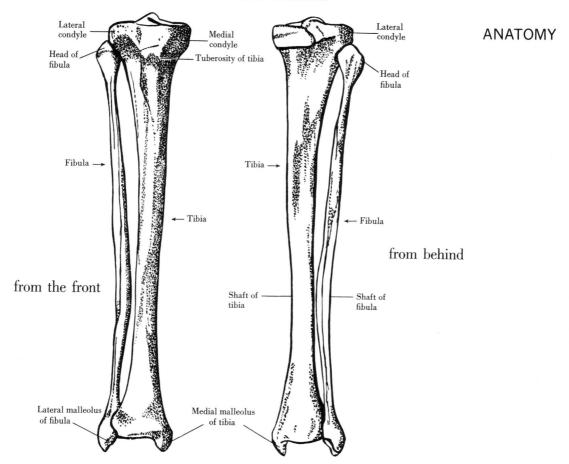

Lateral
condyle

Medial
condyle

Head of
fibula

Tuberosity of tibia

Lateral
condyle

Head of
fibula

Fibula →

Tibia →

← Tibia

← Fibula

from behind

from the front

Shaft of
tibia

Shaft of
fibula

Lateral malleolus
of fibula

Medial malleolus
of tibia

and he can peel a banana but can't play the piano or type, even though he has five fingers! (See p. 66.)

Almost every art store has plaster casts of hands and feet. These are valuable to have to study and to draw from.

The leg, like the arm, has three main bones. The upper leg bone is the femur. The two lower leg bones are called the tibia and the fibula. These two bones, fortunately for us, do *not* rotate one over the other like the two lower arm bones.

Anatomy is a vast and almost staggering subject; the interplay of muscles, how they look when tensed and when relaxed, the changes that take place in various positions. Books could be written on this subject and have been. For you I have tried to make a simple synopsis of what I feel you need to know as beginners.

As I finish this little chapter, which I hope will be helpful, I am sitting near an open window overlooking a small, circular pool. In the pool are mirrored the moon and the stars. If God gives a tiny pool the power to reflect the infinity of the heavens, so perhaps to every human soul He has given the ability to reflect what he sees of truth and beauty. May you in your work capture something of the infinite.

# Chapter 5

## SIMPLE PLASTER CASTING

The simplest way to make a plaster cast is to pick up the telephone and say "Come and get it!" Many professional sculptors live through their whole lives without ever knowing how to make the simplest cast because they live in big cities where there are professional plaster-casters to do their work, and, indeed, to be an expert caster is in itself a life work. However, I think it is very valuable to be able to make a simple waste mold because you may find yourself in a remote spot where plaster-casting is unknown.

Once when my husband was sent out by Mr. Ickes as a special consultant for the Department of the Interior, we found ourselves on a remote Navajo Indian Reservation in Arizona. I attended the Tribal Council meetings with him and the more I observed the majestic dignity and powerfully defined bone structure of the Navajo, the more anxious I became to do the head of one. I had no tools, I had no clay, I had no armature, but I had a great urge. One day, driving with our government interpreter through the Blue Canyon, I saw an Indian, horseback, whose profile silhouetted against the sunset seemed to me to be "My Indian," to exemplify in its fierce nobility those qualities of the Navajo that I had been observing and longing to attempt to capture. He was a long-haired Indian, he spoke no English, but our interpreter made him understand my wishes. It took a lot of "powwow" because the Navajo believes likenesses of them carry off their spirit, and they think they will become weak and die! My husband visited the Holy Man of the tribe. The arrangements were all made and Hosteen Wanika agreed to come to the Indian Agency and sit for his portrait. I got the children at a nearby mission to dig clay out of the river bed, untreated, of course, and full of gravel. My armature was made out of a coat hanger. I used a nail file and an orange stick, and, the best tools of all, my fingers, and I modelled his head. What a model he was, never moving, never speaking, silent, magnificent. One day, as I worked, he rose to his majestic height, strode across the room, and picked up my hand! I was paralyzed with terror! I could feel my scalp getting looser and looser but I knew that Indians have a contempt for cowardice in any form so I decided to die there, looking him in the eye! He put my hand on his nose, then he walked over to the head and put his fingers on one nostril. It was a criticism. Working in a poor light, I had foreshortened one nostril, made it smaller than the other, and he observed it with the eyes of a hawk. I corrected it. I bowed and smiled, he bowed and smiled, and that was that. Remember how I've been telling you to walk around your work, keep comparing one side with another, how important it is. This is one way I learned it. Then, next came the casting problem. I had to go one hundred and fifty miles to Gallup, New Mexico, to get plaster of Paris. I put a very thick mold on the head, left the clay in the inside because I was afraid of its breaking in transit, crated it, and shipped it off to New York.

Seven months later when I returned to the city I went up to Columbia University where my plaster-caster has his studio. There I found that the members of the Physics Department adjacent to the Sculpture Department were terribly excited over the way their geiger counters behaved when my head arrived because the clay inside had a big uranium content! So the Navajos made a big uranium strike, which has been written up in the western papers, and I had a lesson in sculpture and won a competition for an Indian Head for Hobart College where my Navajo in bronze now stands beneath a cottonwood tree on the campus.

At a dinner of the National Sculpture Society sometime later, it was announced that I had won the competition for an Indian Head. The great sculptor, Ivan Mestrovic, was seated at my right. He jumped to his feet and, in the gallant European manner, picked up my hand and kissed it, saying, "Let me be the first to congratulate you!" Of course, I didn't wash that hand for a week! I was so overcome at being congratulated on a piece of my sculpture by Mestrovic I couldn't re-

71

Portrait of a Navajo Indian by the author, now on the campus of Hobart College, Geneva, New York

member any of my French—and had forgotten most of my English! I turned to Mr. Cunningham, who sat at my left, and I said, "Mr. Cunningham, you speak French so beautifully, will you tell Mr. Mestrovic for me that having him congratulate me on a piece of my sculpture is as incredible and thrilling as if someone, years ago, when Harry Truman was a sergeant, had told him that he would live to fire a Five Star General!" I think I had read or heard this somewhere, but, used in this connection, Mr. Mestrovic loved it and it brought down the house.

Mr. Kipling said, "There are nine and sixty ways of constructing tribal lays and every single one of them is right." So with plaster-casting there are many ways—all right.

The head is the simplest to cast. It can be made in two halves. You will require the following equipment: about fifty pounds of the best and finest grade plaster of Paris, two large basins, a stick of blueing, scissors, a bottle of liquid green soap, some burlap (an old potato sack does nicely), chisels, a hammer, pliers, and strips of thin brass or copper about two inches long and one inch wide.

In making a plaster cast, since it is necessary to make a mess and you do not want to make a cast of yourself, cover your hair with a scarf and wear old clothes. Plaster is death to nylons and good shoes; also, you have to abandon your manicure.

73

Cover your floor with a piece of oil cloth or old newspapers, and for chairs, table, stand, whatever you use, the nylon plastic bags that cleaners use for returning your clothes make marvelous coverings. Also, they are invaluable for covering sculpture in wet clay, as the plastic material is light in weight and keeps moisture out.

Put your head at eye level in a good light. Have all your materials handy, as you have to work fast. Cut your burlap into strips eight to ten inches long and about three inches wide.

Fill your basins with cold, clear water. Take one of your modelling tools and with it draw a line back of the ears, which will divide the front from the back half. The ears, if left a part of the front half, are far less likely to get broken off when you separate the two halves of the mold. On the line which you have drawn, begin to press in your little pieces of brass (these are called shims, and roofing concerns sell the thin copper or brass in sheets). As you follow your line around, you find you are giving your head a shining halo! Be sure that the top edges of brass are trimmed so that they form an even edge, no one point sticking up beyond another and no cracks in between.

Into one basin of water drop your stick of blueing. Let it soak in the water until you get a sea blue color, then take it out. Now sift in plaster by stirring with your hand to be sure

74

that there are no lumps in it, and until the bubbles rise to the surface. You get a mixture that is about the consistency of heavy cream. Cover the back half of your head with a rag so it will not get plaster spattered on it. You are now ready to put on your first layer of plaster, which is colored blue so that when you come to chipping out your mold you will go gently, knowing that you are getting close to your inside cast.

With your hands and with an upward motion, begin tossing your plaster onto the front half. Be sure to throw it hard enough so that it will go into the undercuts, eyes, nostrils, ears, etc. Continue until you have a thin coating all over the front half. Now turn your head around, remove the rags, and do the back half in the same way. Be sure at all times throughout the casting process that you keep the top of your brass shims clean of plaster and visible.

Now mix the second basin of plaster without blueing. Let this mixture be thicker. Apply this over the blue layer, always keeping the shims visible, until about two inches thickness has been reached. Now dip your burlap strips into the remaining thick plaster in the bottom of your basin and stick them up and down and crosswise and around the neck to the outside of your mold. The burlap strips serve as reinforcements and will keep your mold from breaking. Some sculptors use irons instead of burlap.

You may be surprised to notice that in a few minutes

75

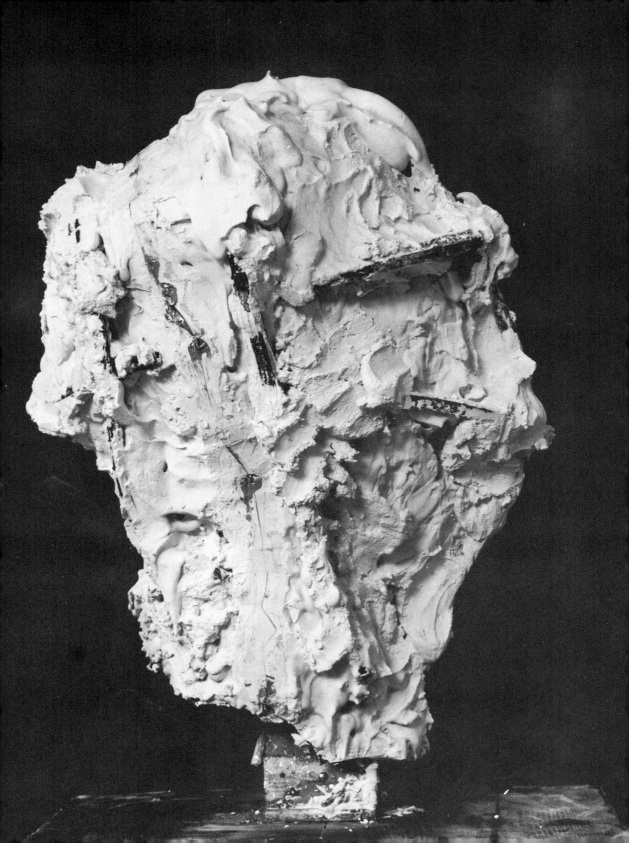

*Above:* Two halves of the mold

*Opposite:* Head covered with plaster, with seams and metal braces showing 77

your plaster begins to get hot. This is a chemical reaction which shows you your plaster is setting.

In about a half hour your mold is ready to be divided. This is the moment for gentle solicitude and care!

With a pair of pliers pull out your pieces of brass, then, standing behind your head, gently work the back half loose. Clean out the clay or plasteline from the back half. Then gently remove the clay or plasteline and the armature from the front half. Be sure both halves are completely clean. You will note that looking down in your mold is like looking at a negative in a photograph. The high points are low, the low areas high. As you clean out your mold be very careful not to scrape the inner surface. Now the two halves must be soaped. Use liquid green soap for this and a soft brush. Soap well but be careful not to leave any bubbles. Let the plaster absorb the soap completely.

Mix another basin full of plaster. Fill both halves with plaster that is well mixed but not too thick. Be sure every crevice is filled. When your molds are filled to a depth of three inches, clap the two halves together. Tie with a rope and put strips of plaster-soaked burlap along the seams if necessary.

It is wise to let your cast set overnight so that it is thoroughly hard and dry.

*Opposite:* Chipping off the mold

With a chisel and hammer, pry loose your burlap strips. Stand your mold upright and start to chip gently. Do not force the chisel in too deeply. Hold the chisel at an angle; do not stick it in straight. Pieces of white plaster will begin to chip off, revealing the inner layer of blue plaster. Begin working at the top and chip downward. Go gently around ears and nose; do not force pieces to come away that seem to want to adhere. Patience at this stage is vital but as the pieces fall off and your cast becomes visible it is very exciting. If you have gouged in too deeply, or you find inequalities and bubbles, don't be discouraged. A cast can look like it has a bad case of smallpox, but wetting spots first and filling in pits with a small brush and freshly mixed plaster is simple and effective.

A dead white cast is never beautiful. A little color will help. Some sculptor, I think Michelangelo, has said, "Clay is the birth, plaster is the death, and marble, the resurrection."

With casein you can make a lovely terra cotta patina: get a tube of Indian red, one of yellow Ochre and one white. Mix these with a brush and water until you get the color you want, then paint it on. Be sure your cast is completely dry before applying any color. An ivory tone can be gotten by using white shellac thinned with one and one half times as much alcohol.

There are many methods of making a bronze patina. One, which Mr. Solon Borglum taught me, that is very effective, I will pass on to you. Shellac your head, allow it to dry, then paint the high points, such as the brow, the ridge of the nose, the chin, the ridges of the ears, with gold paint. Let it dry. At the ten-cent store you can get little bags of dry, powdered paint. Shave beeswax into turpentine, melt in a double boiler until the consistency of butter, be very careful not to catch on fire. Use a very low heat. Cover the head with the melted wax, and with a little rag begin to dot on your powdered colors. Use any color, red, blue, green, brown, black or yellow, and work toward the ultimate tone that you desire. You can make a light green, a dark green, a dark brown, any tone that appeals to you. The more you rub in varying colors the better the result. It may take hours, it may take days. I have never been able to get the exact same color twice but this method does result in a bronze color that is hard to tell from actual bronze. The last step is to dust on talcum powder and rub with something rough, like an old bath towel. The talc adds a metallic burnish.

As I said earlier in this chapter, plaster-casting can be dull but is often vital. I had an experience once that was very amusing. I have a home and studio in the Blue Ridge Mountains of North Carolina, forty miles from a railroad. I had a mountaineer named Hank for a caretaker who took a very dim view of my sculpture. He didn't see "no sense" to me "a-doin' them there statues no way." I had modelled the

81

two grandchildren of Mr. and Mrs. Charles Cannon of Concord, full length and life size, and I was faced with the transportation problem.

Hank asked, "Miss Marjorie, how are you a-aimin' to get that there back to New York?"

"Well, Hank," I replied, "I'll send to Charlotte and get two hundred fifty pounds of plaster and make a thick mold over it and take it north in my car!"

He was very dubious over the whole thing, and when I did have the statue covered with a thick mold and braced with irons so that it looked like an igloo with pipes sticking out of it, he said, "That there h'aint a-goin' to get in no car. Hit'll weigh four hundred seventy five pounds."

"Hank," I said, "that big Packard ought to carry four hundred seventy five pounds on the back seat. Call in the neighbors."

So the farmers round about gathered and dwelt on the problem, spitting tobacco juice in all directions. Finally they took the doors of the car off the hinges, took out the back seat, wormed my mold into the rear, where it was leveled off with bricks like everything else in North Carolina, and I set sail down the mountain. Of course, I couldn't see out of my rear window! Some miles down the road I stopped at a filling station to get some gasoline. There another mountaineer let the gas run all over the road because he was so fascinated with what I had in the car. Finally he came up to me and said,

"Lady, I h'aint one to go a-stickin' my nose into something that just plumb h'aint my business, but I must know what that thar is you got in your automobile. Is it a heating system?"

"Well," I said, "I hadn't thought of it in that way before, but now that you mention it, yes, that's just what it is—it keeps the home fires burning!"

"No," he said, "go on and tell me, sure enough, what that thar is."

"If you must know," I said, "it's art!"

He turned white as a sheet and said, "I've hearn tell of this here modern art, but I h'aint never seed nothing that looks as little like nothing as that thar does. Did you do it yourself?" I didn't have the strength to explain to him that it was like a chicken in the egg—the statue was on the inside!

# Chapter 6

## MODELLING ANIMALS

Winston Churchill has said of painting that to start requires "audacity," and I feel that to succeed at sculpture necessitates a certain self confidence, a form of creative conceit. You have to feel in the beginning that you will succeed, or you are certain to fail. The more difficult the problem the more one needs to feel capable to cope with it. In undertaking to model animals the prime requisite seems to be a love of animals. The great pieces of animal sculpture show the love as well as the knowledge that the artist has of the animal. Women particularly seem to have the ability to show love for animals in their work. Anna Hyatt Huntington, Katherine Weems, Gertrude Lathrop and Madeline Park are among our fine animal sculptors. Mrs. Park loved animals so that she went to Africa to study them in their native habitat. She brought wild animals back as pets. She followed circuses from town to town. She died at the circus with a bag of peanuts in her lap! What a happy way to go, doing what you love best, which with her was to study animals.

I do not want here in a book for beginners to go into the anatomical details but I do not want you to think any

Malvina Hoffman's *Reaching Panther*

animal from a chipmunk to an elephant can be done without a knowledge of anatomy. A round ball on paws is not a kitten. You have to know the bone structure, the muscular structure. It is fascinating to see the comparison between the human skeleton and that of the animal—animals, even birds, all have pelvic bones, vertebrae, scapulas, and arms (in the case of birds, wing bones), and, in the quadruped, front legs and skulls.

Build your armature from a central pipe which should go through the center of the animal. Do not make your legs attached rigidly to your base board as you will want to change the position often.

Study the action of the animal and then try to analyze the main intangible quality of personality of that particular animal—the speed of the horse, the ferocity and power of the lion, the stealth of the great cats, the grace of the deer, the playfulness of the kitten, and so forth. An animal with short hair is best to start with as the bones and planes are seen more readily. In even the heavy-coated animals, such as the bear, study the varying planes of the masses of fur. No scratching on the surface will give the illusion of fur. Study how the fur grows. One mass may move in exactly the opposite direction from another. These planes make fascinating patterns which give the illusion of fur without any surface technique to imitate fur.

I have before me a bronze by the great French animal sculptor, Baryè. Here seated, tense with excitement which you can feel quivering over his whole body, is a hound dog.

Baryè's hound and turtle

In front of him is a turtle, an oblivious turtle. The dog has as much of his ears raised as hounds can raise their ears. The expression of his face, his whole attitude, is one of intense interest and excitement. This small statue is a joy to me, for here the sculptor has done what he set out to do—captured a mood and a moment of life and given it immortality.

So, love your subject, know your subject, study it in action, and get to work!

# Chapter 7

## IMAGINATIVE COMPOSITION

It is not necessary for the student, the beginner, to understand the ramifications of bronze-casting and of marble-cutting. It is important, though, to know that all sculpture goes through three phases—clay, plaster, and then bronze or marble. Do not make the mistake one lady made when she picked up my hand and said, "What a little hand to work in bronze." Don't make the mistake of another lady, looking at a head carved in marble, who asked me, "How long does it take a thing like this to harden?"

Bronze-casting is a highly specialized and intricate procedure. The molten metal is poured into a mold. There are experts in the various types of casting, sand-casting, and the "cire perdue" or "lost wax" process. All you have to do is turn your plaster cast over to a bronze foundry, of which there are many, and they will do the casting job for you. You may want to supervise the patina, which is done with acids and a blow pipe. Bronze can be any tone—black, brown, green, "verde antique," or golden—the color is a matter of taste.

BRONZE CASTING

As for marble, there are those to whom the stone speaks, like Michelangelo. Carving direct in stone is rare.

MARBLE
CARVING

Usually the marble is carved from a design in plaster. You can employ a professional carver who will reproduce your plaster model through the use of a mechanical device known as a pointing machine, which takes hundreds of measurements. Rasps, sandpaper, chisels are used for polishing and finishing, but stone-carving is in itself a study beyond the field of the beginner unless that beginner is a rarely talented one with an instinctive "feel for stone."

Good practice for the student who wants to know what it is like to carve is to get a large laundry-size cake of Ivory soap. Draw your design on the surface and then begin to cut back, using a sharp knife or plaster tool. Nothing can be added back on, so that in using a cheap material you can practice direct carving and still have soap flakes to spare!

GROUPING
FIGURES

In grouping figures, the sculptor must consider the mass as a whole and this mass is based on a geometric form. Your group may have as its underlying structure a pyramid, a square, a circle, or a spiral. An interesting way of studying the geometric pattern of works of art is to get some tracing paper, put it over some elaborate composition, such as one of Botticelli's paintings, trace the main lines, and you will find the underlying geometric basis of the composition. You will find emphasis given by the use of repetition. The sculptor must remember mass. Volume is important. The idea your design expresses is of course the most important thing but,

Botticelli's *Adoration of the Magi*

to express it well in sculpture, its basis must exist in a geometric form.

Often a pile of discarded plasteline, lying neglected on a table, will suddenly, in a certain light and shade, suggest groups of figures or give you an idea for a composition. I remember once that damp cloths wrapped around a wet clay model in the twilight of my studio suddenly, for me, became a group of figures. Fronds of ferns in the woods seemed to me

*Above: Lovers—The Prayer* by Malvina Hoffman illustrates imaginative composition.

*Opposite: Frond Fountain,* by the author

one day to develop faces and moved me to model a frond fountain based on nature's spiral composition revealed in unfurling ferns. Clouds can be monuments. The imagination can be stimulated by so many things! It is the artist who transmutes the commonplace into the extraordinary. "Beauty is in the eye of the beholder." It is the mission of the artist to share his vision, to open the eyes of all to the beauty which he perceives, to the perfection of design from the smallest seashell to the spiral nebulae.

Let your work be a revelation of how you think, of how you feel, of what you see around you, and you will have achieved a deep joy in creating it, a widened awareness of the world about you, a deep understanding that there is a force moving through you as a tool that is not you yourself. Your understanding of the works of others will be far greater for having stepped forth on the broad highway of creative expression.

> "All passes, Art alone enduring stays to us.
> The bust outlasts the throne.
> The coin, Tiberius."

*Opposite: The Spirit of American Youth* by Donald De Lue, at Normandy (France) American Cemetery

# Acknowledgments

Alinari: pp. 31, 48, 53, 60–61

American Battle Monuments Commission: p. 94

Author: jacket photograph; pp. 13, 22, 23, 24, (sitter, George M. Ivey); 72, 87 (photograph by Peter A. Juley and Son), 92 (photograph by Peter A. Juley and Son)

Bethlehem Steel Company: p. 17

The British Travel Association: p. 58

Courtesy of Mrs. H. Frank Forsyth, (photograph by Peter A. Juley and Son): p. 35

Georgetown University, (photograph by Peter A. Juley and Son): p. 39

Courtesy of Mrs. Albert Gins: p. 34

Courtesy of Miss Malvina Hoffman: pp. 85, 93

The Metropolitan Museum of Art: p. 33 (Lazurus Fund, 1914); 52 (Rogers Fund, 1933); 85 (Gift of Archer M. Huntington, 1925)

National Gallery of Art, Washington, D. C., Mellon Collection: p. 91

National Capital Parks Commission: p. 55

The Oriental Institute, University of Chicago: p. 30

Royal Commission on Historical Monuments (England): p. 59 (Copyright The Rev. P. Sumner)

Courtesy of Ettore Salvatore, (photograph by Walter J. Russell): pp. 76, 77, 78

Sculpture House, Inc.: p. 44